CHAPTER ONE

According to you what is life? A dull depressed phenomenon or a enthusiastic energetic expansion.

Actually it depends upon the individual. How he takes it.Body perceives this world through the help of his senses.Senses gives the projection of external world to the inner mind.Mind process the data given by the senses through the prism of his subconscious mind.Mind generates thoughts , feelings and emotions.Thoughts comes and goes within the mind creating a zone of inner content within us. Our entire planet earth is inhabited by seven billion individuals who thinks in the same basic pattern . They actually live in a domain of thoughts forming the same collective mind.Thoughts needs language to operate upon and there are so many languages in this world. Thoughts creates a movement within our mind and forms the impressions of this world. So our entire physical world throbs and feel in the form of mind. This mind created war , crime , depression , peace , love and kindness. All the good and bad in this world is the creation of our mind.So our mind is the great cosmic problem and also it is great cosmic solution also.It is a dynamic process and a great phenomenon.It is the product of evolution of this universe and it

has all the properties and mystic abilities of this universe.Problem with us is that we are not able to ascend normal domain of thoughts within us. We do not understand that the energy beyond thoughts within us can expand and contract.
This expansion and contraction of mind is the subject matter of study.Through certain technique of meditation and mysticism our entire inner being can expand to a higher dimension. This propelling force is the essence of our being.
How to unfold the energies propelling within us. With the practice of meditation this energy can unfold itself and can grow into higher dimensions.

CHAPTER TWO

SCIENCE OF MANTRA

Science of mantra is science of sound vibrations.To understand this we have to understand the entire science of sound , its meaning and its effect on our inner energies and consciousness. Any word that we speak has got a sound like characteristic and a meaning attached with it. But basically any sound wave is first of all a sound first. Sound is a form of vibration .

In science of mantra there are certain sound waves which has a great effect on our inner consciousness. These are known as seed mantra because if proper environment is given to these seed mantra then they can sprout into a great tree of wisdom and change in consciousness. Our ancient rishis have utilised this vibrational property of sound to create a change in our inner consciousness.

To understand this we have to understand the sound and vibrational properties of omkar. The word omkar is made up of three sounds A, U and M. Three sounds in the word omkar signifies our three state of consciousness that is waking , dreaming and sleeping and the silence after omkar signifies the fourth state of consciousness that is turiya . So in the science of mantra power of sound vibration is used to expand our consciousness in higher dimensions.

If you want to practice this great science then do a basic practice of chanting omkar.

Omkar chanting energies our inner consciousness.It expands our inner world.In the great practice of sri vidya tantra seed mantra is used to energies our centre of consciousness.

CHAPTER THREE

MIRACULOUS ASPECTS OF MIND

Life is full of situations and circumstances which are miraculous and mystic in nature. You desire something , you crave for something , you try and it happens as a reality for you. Sometimes it doesn't happens according to your wishes , then you get disheartened.

Whenever you feel disheartened always remember all the power of universe lies in your mind.Your mind is seat and epicenter of all the miracles of this universe. You can manifest anything if your consciousness is expanded.Expanded mind is the most magnificent thing in this world.
To understand the mind we should first of all understand the nature of mind.What is mind? Mind is always coagulated with thoughts.Thoughts come and go inside our mind and we are always absorbed with this world.Is there anything inside us which is beyond thoughts.This is state of consciousness. These

are waking , dreaming and sleeping.
Now the most important mystic question arises from here that is , is there any other state of consciousness other than waking , dreaming and sleeping. For that we have to explore the nature of our mind.We have to understand the expansion and contraction of consciousness within us.Expanded mind can traverse any levels of existence within us. The power of manifestation increases manifold inside us.This power of manifestation can lead to many forms of miracles for us.How this entire world of miracles operates before us.We should have to understand this entire mechanism.Since our

desires are materialistic in nature we have to understand the nature of materialistic reality. All the nature of materialistic reality are in the form of vibrations.When we look deep inside the nature of material world we find that matter is actually made up of electrons , protons and neutrons which are constantly in state of movement.Furthermore matter is actually a form of energy.This energy is vibrating in every matter.Our mind is also vibrating in certain frequency.When we can atune our mind to certain higher vibratory states then we can touch the higher domain of reality operating within us.

All the matter that we see is actually a condensed form of consciousness.In expanded state of consciousness materialization become more easy.
But the basic question is still there that is how to expand your state of consciousness. For this you have to use some of the primitive fountain of life within us. For example we can use our breathe as a vehicle of consciousness.Our breath is closely associated with the inner pranic energy within us.This pranic energy is closely attached to the pool of consciousness within us. For this the basic mantra is soham. With the inspiration chant so in your mind and with expiration chant hum in

your mind . On conatantly doing this slowly and slowly you will find that a spark of joy is arising in your mind and you are becoming more and more silent. There is one more effective method of mystic practice.That is chanting of omkar which has got great effect on our consciousness. Take a deep inspiration and with the current of expiration chant omkar.This prolong sound of omkar creates a expansion of consciousness within you.This expanding mind is the greatest miracle operating within you.

Effect of sound waves to relax our mind and creating a positive effect on our consciousness is most effective method of expansion of mind.Every sound wave has got a form attached with it and that sound form has got a great effect on the pool of consciousness within us.

So when external world irritates you then try to go inside and find something more concrete and great in your inner world of consciousness. Always remember inside you are a miracle as massive as this entire universe.This universe has got its birth from the great power of consciousness.This power of consciousness is the most magnificent entity in this world. Problem with us is that we are always involved in the gross domain of thoughts only.We are trapped in a box.We think in a

box.We feel helpless and trapped. Negative thoughts have created a block in our state of consciousness.But our nature is freedom.Inside we want to free ourself.

So focus on something which is near to some primitive fountain within us.

As a medical student I was always exposed to various facets of health and diseases, and I have always a curiosity to understand the concept of holistic health. A symbolism of health in which we find a perfect balance of body , mind , thought , emotions , feelings and past memories. But in practical world I always find apparently healthy people surrounded by great deal of mental turmoil or I find people having both physical and mental illness. Whole of medical sciences, drugs , treatment modules cannot give us what we are craving for, that is, complete physical and mental wellbeing.

My mind was burning with questions and my medical books were not able to give satisfactory reply of my questions, that I was always asking. Then opened a new chapter in my life that is , chapter of inner observation or meditation which gave me replies to the many questions , I was seeking for.

Meditation opened before me a complete world of physical and mental well being. A journey of silence and peace.

After realizing the benefit of basic art of inner observation, I was motivated to write a book on the ***mystic*** and ***miraculous*** aspect of meditation.

During the process of creation of this book , I have taken keen precaution that each and every word should be written in deep silence and peace, so that essence of meditative practices should be reflected in every word.

CHAPTER ONE

“CONDITIONS OF MIND AND RESISTANCES WE FACE IN OUR INTERNAL WORLD”

If you have a keen desire to know your real self , then try to sit a room all alone, silently and peacefully. Look at the thoughts and feelings coming and going within your mind. When you will sit quietly and observe every changes going on within you, then try not to attach yourself with any of the phenomenon happening within your mind. Try to observe every bit of motion happening in our inner core with detachment.

You will observe a train of thoughts ,images , past memories arising within you, which will give birth to the feeling of either pain or pleasure within you. Every thought that comes and go creates a imprint on our mind in the form of pain and pleasure. They are like ripples on steady water.

Now the purpose of meditation is to settle the whirlpool of events occurring in our mind. But we cannot suppress any thought within us, it is against our natural law of our mind. Suppressed thought come out in form of dreams within us.

Constant observation of our mind can lead us to some degree of tranquilty within us. But if you really want to go beyond the domain of mental movements, then we should have an understanding of various modalities of our mind.

In a life of 24 hours, our mind moves into three states of consciousness that are Waking , dreaming and sleeping. Our entire life is engrossed within these states of consciousness.

In waking state, all of our sensory apparatus get opened up to receive stimulus from the external world like eyes, ears , tongue and skin or in other words, Sight , sound , smell and taste. They are the medium to receive stimulus from the external world and give this information to our internal world. Our internal world tries to interpret this stimulus and this is called *Intellect*. Intellect always tries to function in tandem with our inner identity i.e. known as Ego. Our sense of inner identity has a property of inertia i.e. it wants to retain itself. Ego tries to separate our intellect from our real spiritual identity.

In a nutshell in waking state of consciousness , senses gives data to intellect which functions according to our ego. This creates an entire aura of movement of waking state.

When we move in our dream state, then input of data from sensory take a pause because our senses are not working in our dream state. Dream creates a entire new world within us from our subconscious without the help of our senses. We live , feel and express in ourself in our dreams as in same manner as in awake state without the help of senses. During that moment dream is as real as waking state. It is like reality within reality different from the original world.

Then slowly mind goes into deep aura of sleep where every moment of mind goes away and what is left is nothingness without any awareness. But remember , sleep doesnot have any transforming property. A fool goes into sleep and come out as a fool. But sleep has got an energizing property within us. When we wake from sleep our mind function in more energetic manner. If we donot sleep for 1 to 2 days , we cannot function in waking state.

Now the question arises that are there only three states of consciousness within us? Or there is some more expandable and worthy state of consciousness which has a transforming property?

In deep meditation our consciousness expands and it pierces our conscious and subconscious mind and goes into a state which is more blissful and peacefull. Actually we live in planes of reality of waking , dreaming and sleeping. And with our conscious effort we can go into more expandable state. This starts infinite journey of looking within , searching within and finding within.

When I started my practice of meditation I keenly observed that our consciousness is made up of energy states known as pranik energies. During meditation , pranik energies increases within us which leads to better control and settlement of our mind. Still mind can explore this domain of pranik energies. For this we should try to become a keen observer of our inner self.

CHAPTER TWO

PREPARATION OF MEDITATION

One of the most basic question of this discussion is that , inspite of meditation being cure of all problems of life. Why it is very difficult for people to follow? Why maximum people of this world are not able to involve themselves into meditative wisdom?

Answer lies in the preparation of meditation. Preparation is more tougher than the act of meditation. Preparing yourself for the meditative practices need a balance in five primitive fountains of life , these are food, sleep , sexuality , self preservation and breath. The unified energy that we experience in meditation are combined resultant of these basic five fountains. Balancing these forces within us can help us to expand our mind. We will discuss each of these fountains separately. FOOD: what we donot realize in our life is that food ultimately become part of our mind. Food depends upon two factors : quality and quantity. If quality of food is more spicy then it will create an agonizing effect on our mind. Mild and modest foods like fruits and milk will pacify our mind. Every food item create transient effect our mental virtues. Alcohol and marijuana creates a deluding effect.

Hunger is one of the most primitive force of human existence. The first cry of a baby is for food only. Force of hunger if properly dealt can expand our mind. That's why fasting is one of the most basic component of every religion of this world. So what we want to prove is that controlling hunger and modifying food can create a change in grooves of mind. Maximum of our habit patterns are related to food which forms deep impression in content of our mind.

SEXUALITY: sexuality both as external act and internal imagination can create a burst of transient ecstasy within us which ultimately results into drain out phenomenon. Sexuality is that great primitive force which has given birth to entire planet. This force if analysed properly and balanced can lead to more clairyonce and balance in our internal world. Sexual joy is a transient reflection of higher form of consciousness within us. There is joy in sexuality but it doesn’t expand. We are in a search of more expandable joy. We want to convert a draining out phenomenon of sexuality into expanding phenomenon of meditation.

Sexuality proves that, through certain methodology and imaginative patterns , our mind can move into ecstatic transient joy, but it doesn't expand. So we are in search of joy that can be sustained, which is possible by controlling this force of sexuality.

Sleep: try to do a experiment with your mind, select a day and take a lot of money , and do everything that pleases you, like adulterants , sexuality ,good food etc. after enjoying every object that you can, there will be a time when you just want to sleep.

All the joys of this world and ample money cannot replace sleep. If you are not able sleep for a single day, you are able to operate properly in waking state. Important question that arises here is that what is there in sleep which cannot be replaced by all the joys of this world. Answer is that all the joys ultimately drain us,but sleep re- energize us. We are able to enjoy this world from the energies of sleep only. Do any joyful act repeatedly you will find yourself drained and ultimately you will sleep. So logically sleep is greatest joy of this world. So any reenergizes act which can replace sleep can be greatest ecstasy of this world. Meditation is that act, in deep meditation we donot feel like sleeping and we are never drained out.

Self preservation: it is one of the most difficult part of meditative practices. Self within us is always in fear of loosing something. Whether it is career, money , health , family . our mind is in constant fear which drains energy of our mind. Overcoming this fear is very essential for getting a clear and pure mind. This can only be done by strong philosophical foundations.
One everything has to end, so why we are becoming so possessive

about it. So why to create a resistance of fear within our mind. We have to analyse each and e very blockage within our mind and have to find a philosophical solution.

Breath:breath and mind are like twin brothers. Every change in our breath will be reflected in our mind and vice versa. When we are in grief our beath becomes shallow and when we are happy our breath become deeper. We laugh in full domain of expiration. So by creating a change in our breath we can create change in our mind. When breath become balanced then mind synergerize with it. That's why brathing practices have always been a base of yogic sciences. The day we realize that our consciousness depend upon these basic fountains , we will sorry state for ourself because they are not balanced. The day we balance these basic fountains we find ourself in expanded state of consciousness.

Chapter 3
CONCEPT OF GOD

Definition of GOD is one of the most central concept in theory of religion. Every religion understand god in their own unique way. Some try to find god in idol.in prophets ,in religious sign, in heaven but there should be some concrete definition of god, that no body has. We have to analyse god from an analytical hypothesis. W

Whatever be our concept of god, let that object or prophet or heaven get materialized in front of us. Then what we will do with that materialization? What a human being can ask from such a hypothetical god. In think his desires first of all, like money , relation , property etc. after satisfaction of his desires , he will ask for happiness. After happiness a human being will ask anything that can fulfill his unfullfillment within him. So overall human being wants to expand himself from materialistic desires to happiness to something more that fulfill him. It is an unending journey that has no destination. So that anything that can satisfy this vaccum in human being is actually is god. Whether it is idol or prophet or anything else.

This question can be analysed in one more prospect. Why we need god?. Answer is because we are unhappy , sad and we want something or there are lot questions in our mind.

When a yogi goes deep inside in him, then first of all he has to fight with forest of thoughts within him. Thoughts are reflection of spark of desires. These desires have a magnetism of attachment within them. When you observe your thought without attachment ,then you cross realm of thought and mind goes into ocean of bliss within himself. This deeper state is replies of all the questions that we are asking for. All of our desires are satisfied in this spark of divinity. This deep inner state has everything that we are asking from god. So there is state within us which has all the components of satisfaction and expansion that we crave from god. So inside us there is god which is beyond the realm of desires, thoughts , emotions and embedded in the ocean of bliss.

So search of god that starts from the outside world get its reply from something within us. A state of mind where there are no questions can be found within us. This is a big hope for our life. So ultimately it is an ancient wisdom of looking within , searching within and finding within.

How much we can go inside? What is the limit ? actually there is no limit. It is journey not a destination. Journey of infinite, endless enriching , fulfulling and expanding always. External world is reflection of our internal self. Anything that happens outside, first of all occur inside. Every action is subtle thought, so if there is worship of god outside then there must be subtle essence of god inside also and that lies in deeper state of meditation.

CHAPTER 4
ANALYSING THE ENERGY WITHIN

The utmost need of spiritual process is to analyse the energy state within us.Spiritual aspirant should be aware of all of his states from sleeping , waking to dreaming.How the mind moves into these states is the subject matter of spirituality.

Understanding these states opens the new avenue of this mind.Mind is our greatest enemy and also it is our greatest friend.Energy states creates such a rainbow within us that it becomes soo much difficult to decifer.

The entire inner being which is the subject matter of our study is known as consciousness . It moves into various states and various forms.It is in everybody but we are not able to understand it and most important for many of us we are not able to expand it through various method of meditation and mysticism.Deep within us there is ocean of knowledge which is untouched by many of us.

Energy state that we are able to understand has got many denominations , and it moves from one level to another.

Lower levels of energy states are hugely materialistic in nature and they revolve around jumbled pattern of thoughts . When we move more deeper within ourself then potential of imagination develops within us.It is symbolized by the moon. .Moon is symbolism of imagination. Imagination is a greater force within us.It has got a potential to get materialise. Many books have been written on materialization of imaginative forces within us.

These forces should be analyzed very properly before doing any practices of meditation. These are very powerful forces. These forces are essence of our being . They remove the insecurities and cravings constantly happening within the human being.

But the question that arises from here is that how to master these energies. How to become more empowered . To master these energies first of all we have to remove the distractions occurring within the human mind. Chattering

mind should be silenced before going deep inside us.
What is mind actually. It is just movement of thoughts in soo many dimensions, with images of past memories and visuals , that too in very much jumbled manner. This distraction should be worked out .
Mind should be silenced and analyzed very properly to move into these kind of practices. These energies are actually domains of consciousness which moves into various grades and forms. We can easily assess it in the depth of our mind. Lower level of energies operates in thinking domain , deeper within us there is another domain known as domain of visualization in which our imagination works. If mind is very much stronger then imagination acquires the domain of materialization .There is another force within us that is known as force of desire and passion.
There is another great force within us that is known as compassion or emotion . In deep state of emotion , the feeling absorbs our entire inner being . Above these forces there

are undifferentiated forces of spiritual energy that operates within us.

We become acquinted to these higher forces in our deeper state of mind and consciousness. Primary requirement for all these to happen is deep , peaceful and tranquil mind. From here the journey starts. Layer by layers we go deep into our inner recess of mind and we are able to know our true and essential nature.

In spirituality there are soo many methods and process like , meditation , mantra , yoga , fasting. Purpose of all these spiritual methodology is to settle down the monkey mind. Once a tranquil mind is achieved then things become more simple for us. From a tranquil mind we can move into more higher level of consciousness.

Inner states are soo much joyful that it takes the mind in the higher zone of ecstacy. This ecstasy should be enjoyed in deep meditative states. It is like joy of the joy. But constant effort is needed . This field is as much specialized as any other field. According to bhagawat gita constant effort and detachment is essential to become successful in this field.

Also it does not operates like any special mechanism . In our day to day life it operates in a similar manner. If any pleasurable thing absorbs our mind then we move into deep state of meditation. Absorption of mind into pleasurable thing makes us free from the routine conditioning of our mind and we become free. This freedom is internal and it is real and true freedom. It is the freedom about which true spiritual seeker craves for. This is the

Whole life we are engrossed into sensual pleasures . We eat , we sleep , we drink , we do sex .We drain our life and ultimately no option is left than to go into deep state of sleep . Our definition of joy is very narrow. To get more and more joy people land themselves into the world of addiction. Spiritual pleasure in deep state of meditation is the greatest joy that a human being can experience. People with real understanding of wisdom are craving to attain that greatest joy. But the condition is that we have to delve into deep ocean of meditation to understand this entire concept . Meditate , meditate , meditate

, till the higher ocean of wisdom become very much evident for us.
On deep understanding it become very clear that this huge cosmos in material term is nothing but vibration of consciousness . Thus when we develop control over the higher aspect of consciousness then we develop control over material aspect of life. Control over material aspect is very necessary for attaining success in life. People always make a notion that spirituality is a alien science while this world is materialistic . This notion is completely wrong . Truth is that spiritual and material world is very much inter related. As ice , water and vapour is one and the same thing , in the same manner spirituality and material world is one and the same but only there forms are different.

My purpose of writing this book is to make readers aware about greater glory of mind and inner consciousness. Being a medical practitioner what I really feel is that mind is most misunderstood subject in our present academic world. Even psychology is not that much evolved to understand the mind fully. Deeper within us our inner being is far more greater and glorious that we can not imagine. This book is about to analyse phychology in it's various aspect .

Grossly analysing our existence has got two major aspect , one is physical body and other is mind. Physical body has been read and analysed a lot by medical sciences but mind has always been a mystery and still a mystery for genuine reader and psychological scientist. Mind is origin of everything , from god to

crime to agony to frustration. Every good and bad component of human civilization has it's origin in deeper aspect of our mind.
From ancient civilization to modern world still the mystery continues. Purpose of this book is to demystify the things as far as possible. Great psychological suffering and violence has always affected humanity. Origin of gross aspect of problems lies in deeper aspect of mind and consciousness.
It is the topic that should be taken very seriously . Origin of some of the greatest problems of our civilization lies in mind. Origin of religion , spirituality, creativity, everything lies in our mind.
These things should be part of our education , but unfortunately they are not. We are living in a world where everything is soo much confused and

chaotic. They is no direction and orientation on which we can rely ourself. In this gloomy and confusing situation , somewhere deep inside our mind there is a great ocean of solutions and answers . Our purpose is to go deep into that ocean and find some concrete answers for yourself. Our readers are advised to analyse and interpret my writing and try to think in a independent manner so that you can land yourself into certain very concrete and consolidated conclusions.

CHAPTER ONE

NATURE OF MIND AND IT'S MODALITIES

Even the word mind cannot explain what the mind is all about . There are various connotations associated with it , one is brain , other is psychology , then nervous system . First of all we will try to make a very clear concept of all these connotations. See brain is wiring of neurons and mind is energy flowing within it. Though mind operates through neurons but it is entirely different from connections of neurons. Analysing deeply we understand that whole of our body is in mind but whole of our mind is not in our body. Mind is entirely different and vast than whole of our body and neurons.

In order to holistically understand everything just sit in a room and try to observe your mind and the content operating within it. When you will

look at your mind you will find that it is always full of thoughts and chattering domain of thinking pattern . Then sometimes past memories with images comes and effect our inner aspect of being. Within that thought and images emotions flow and absorb the entire inner content of our being. Emotions have the tendency to absorb everthing . Overall there is a chaotic environment inside. Nothing is in control inside our mind that is why nothing is in control in our external environment also. Internal and external environment are replica of each other. This all happens when we are awake and is in our waking state of consciousness . then suddenly state of our consciousness changes and we move into other domain of dreaming state . In dreaming state none of our senses operates but we are able to live in a individual world of ourself. Even without the help of our senses we can live in a inner world of our own . This world is as real as external world. Dreaming reality is far more subjective than waking reality. Dream world constitute subconscious domain of our existence. Then we move into deep sleep when everything become silent and our existence chamges. Again we woke up and see this world .

Question that arises from here is that is this much is our overall domain of existence or there is anything else. A jumbled and chaotic mind and three state of consciousness. From here a subtle observation should start . When we woke up in the morning then our mind is more fresh and energetic .We are able to perform our duty with more clearity. Slowly and slowly after hours of day's activity we become tired and tired. Clearity of our thinking gets clouded after full day activity . Thus our mind contracts from morning to evening. At evening time it become dull and tired and goes to sleep. Thus on close observation it proves that our inner being expands and contracts after a full day of activity. Thus there is something within us which expands and contracts depending upon the circumstances. This expanding and contracting reality is a matter of study for true student of mysticism. It is a great hope of humanity that through certain psychological process our mind can be expanded and contracted.

Before understanding this concept what is really important is that what happens when our limited mind takes a expanded existence. When during

expansion mind expands then the realization of reality changes for us. Expanded mind analyses reality in a entirely different manner.

Next question is that how we can expand our mind. What is the mechanism for expansion of mind. What is tha actual psychological process behind it.

Answer is that meditation is the process of expansion of mind. In expanded state solution of many problems of life become very easy. According to ancient mystic tradition when we go deep inside us we can apprehend fourth state of consciousness that is different from waking , dreaming and sleeping state of consciousness. In the fourth state of consciousness mind can apprehend things in a very different manner. Sensory data that we accumulate from this world does not

affect us any more in this fourth state of consciousness. Thus it is a great hope that our mind can ascend into different dimension of glory and creativity.

Mostly we are not able to ascend to this path but by constant efforts our mind can change the dimension of existence. Always remember friends that our well being begins with the state of mind. If state of mind can be transformed then our grades of existence improves. Thus analysis of state of mind is very essential for analysis of truth. Deeper within us there is throbbing sensation of truth that signifies higher grades of existence within us.

This journey of mind goes far and wide. In a nutshell distracted mind should be focussed and casted into a mould. Then this mould should be shed down and higher reality should be perceived.

CHAPTER TWO
WHAT IS YOGA AND IT'S EIGHTFOLD PATH

After analysing the mind we should know that what to do with a peaceful mind. Peaceful mind can be ascended and united with cosmic consciousness. Yoga is the method of uniting our limited mind with higher expanded state of consciousness . In english language meaning of the word yoga is union with higher state of consciousness. It is known as eightfold path because there is eight

discipline of yoga. These eightfold discipline is known as yama , niyama , asana , pratyahara , Dhyana , dharana and samadhi.
First of all discipline of mind is essential . Discipline of mind always comes with discipline of body. Our thinking pattern first of all should be modulated. Our behaviour , fooding pattern should be analysed and regulated. When all the conflict of food , thinking , sleep and sexuality is wisely regulated then starts the journey of higher expanded state of consciousness. Dephth of our mind then starts new chapter that is delwing into cosmic consciousness. Only a well prepared mind and body can prepare himself to go into the land of cosmic consciousness. After that we are prepared to sit into a posture. Then the energy of senses which is moving outward is taken

into dephth of our being. This phenomenon is known as pratyahara. After conserving of our energy we move into state of mind in which all of our energies are moving in one direction. This is known as meditation . In meditation our entire mind component is absorbed and there is sense of absorption and completeness within ourself. In that state everthing looks soo beautiful. It gives a great meaning to our life. Eightfold path of yoga is like a heirchy in which we move like a ladder and transcend ourself from normal day to day life of activity and discipline into higher divine state of consciousness. Mind flows into this great type of absorption and finds it's true core. Our entire inner being is affected by mind and it's modalities. Even the lowest ladder of our being

creates a great impact on our divine inner being.
From the very ancient times rishis of india have tried to understand the mind and consciousness. They have done valid experiments on their mind th understand the higher reality . These experiments are known as process of sadhana . In deep state of sadhana or meditation there mind transform into a new reality and understanding. Life acquires a new meaning and values . Most important thing is that meditative mind is miraculous also . A silent , tranquil and expanded mind is like a grace which can grant you anything. In depth of your consciousness there lies a bubble of eternity . You have to tap that bubble through the valid and proper science of meditation. Always remember friends , it is science of consciousness . You can practice it

by your sincere efforts and evolve yourself into higher realm of mental states. Always remember success is never achieved by mere hard work . There is some inner components in our mins which is the sole reason of success generation. Success arises from the depth of internal energy within us. Success of any kind can be generated from the depth of our mind . Whether it is money or peace or anything else. Actually there is no hope for humanity except to understand the science of consciousness. Problems that life field before us is manyfold . From career to health to family . There is no limit for the problems before us . Solution is just the mind . Mind which is expanded , magnificient and glorified.

This expanded mind can do anything and can be taken to various

dimensions . The answers , the solutions and the replies that humanity is seeking for centuaries lies in the depth of our mind and consciousness . So attend yourself more and more . Create more awareness within yourself , so that you can ascend to the path of higher consciousness. This field is a very specialize field . It is the way to understand god and eternity . Psychology is not mere a science but it is the doorway to the higher reality. Our mind should be silent and tranquil to understand this higher reality . This ascended mind should be seat of pure thought and pure habits . Only then it's importance is realised .

In our civilisation people think in a very negative and depressive manner . There faces are dull with hopelessness . Fear of life , disease ,

money and future is always subsiding behind the normal human mind . Internal mind has been so much corrupted that it has given rise to soo much crime and violence in our society . Transforming inner reality is all about transforming our entire civilization . So look within , search within and find within the higher reality that is seeking ourself . According to swami Vivekananda , arise , awake and stop not till the goal of reaching higher expanded reality is achieved and mind ascends from normal existence of humanity to the greater existence of divinity. Yoga with it's eightfold path is a ladder which teaches the same thing . How a disciplined body and mind can absorb itself into higher level of consciousness so that a higher and deeper state of samadhi can be reached.

Try to understand this analogy , you have to reach somewhere and you are changing your path every moment . So you will never reach your destination . In the same manner mind operates . Mind is always distracted , so it never reaches any conclusions . Only after meditative practices our mind becomes one pointed . This one pointed mind can be taken into any destination. This is how prayers work . When we pray before god we always create contradictory statements , so our prayers are never answered . Prayers like child is answered by eternity because child never contradicts what he is feeling . so always pray like a child . Ask the eternity about your feelings in a child like manner . Pose your demands . Believe me , nature will listen to your desires. This is the science and magic of spirituality. Life

is not a bag of miseries but it is gift of eternity and it depends upon the subjective perception of the seeker to understand life in that manner.
This entire civilisation will make you work , work and work and will ultimately drain you out . We have no other option left than go for passive domain of sleep . Is this life ? Living here , eating , sleeping and drinking . Striving to make money and ultimately die one day . This is not what the life is all about . There is something else to this life . This something else is analysed in internal domain of our mind . From here the concept of looking inside have got it's meaning.
These questions goes very much far and wide. It is the source of light within our consciousness. This vibrant light should be seeked out first and then the real meaning of life

should be analysed. People from ancient civilization to modern civilization are trying there best to find this great purpose of life.
This body and mind is just not the physiological mechanism happening within us . It is the massive phenomenon of energy throbbing within us . This massive phenomenon is called divinity and light within us . This throbbing reality is soo much hidden and soo much evident within us . Seeker seek it , knower practices it like a pro. Life posess a question and answers are tough to find . But this is the journe and this is the way . Both the journey and way is within our mind . From the forest of thoughts , emotions and memories go beyond and try to find ultimate reality living within us .

CHAPTER THREE
SIX SYSTEMS OF INDIAN PHILOSOPHY.

This is one of the most beautiful topic that should be read and understood deeply in the field of mysticism.

There are six major school of Indian philosophy . These are nyay , vaisheshikha, samkya , yoga , mimansa and Vedanta.

First of all we will discuss about Nyay school of Indian philosophy. Nyay means judgement. Nyay system of Indian philosophy led to systematic development of theory of logic , methodology and epistemology.

According to Nyay school , There are six reliable means of gaining knowledge , these are perception , inference , comparison , analogy and word. Nyay school of philosophy talks about right knowledge and wrong knowledge . It creates a branch known as epistemiology which talks about what is real and what is unreal . It states that suffering is due to wrong actions and liberation is due to right actions. Correct knowledge is about going into the depth of our mind and finding the true nature of soul and cosmic consciousness within us.

Nyay school believes that all the way in which knowledge is attained are imperfect . senses are imperfect , thinking is imperfect , reasoning is imperfect . Only through deep meditation , what we gain is known as real knowledge.

Vaisheshika school of Indian philosophy was such a dynamic school. In this school scientific concept is discussed very properly. This was such a revolutionary school that described that all the matter that we see is made up of atoms. These atoms are joined with each other through cosmic forces. According to vaisheshika school knowledge and liberation is achieved through complete understanding of world of experience. This school depicts that knowledge can be attained by two means , one is perception and other is inference. World of perception has lot of limitation , this limitation can be overcome by meditating on higher form of reality. Thus higher form of reality can be perceived by deep meditation.

Next school of Indian philosophy that is really vast and great is Samkhya. Meaning of the word Samkhya is enumeration. This philosophy means counting the factors that affects the human beings. Samkhya philosophy asserts that there is groosly two things in this world . One is matter and other is consciousness. Both matter and consciousness creates a play in the individual being . Consciousness has the potential to materialise and matter can dematerialise under the influence of consciousness. This great science was discovered by great rishi Kapila. The literal meaning of word Samkhya is to count. Sankhya wants to calculate all the factor that influence the existence of human being. Katha Upanishad describes Samkhya philosophy in a very poetric manner. It states that higher than senses stands the object of senses , higher than object of senses , stands mind . Higher than mind stands intellect . higher than intellect stands the great self . Higher than great self stands the unmanifested. Higher than unmanifested stands the great purusha. It is only known by the people who think in a very subtle manner. Samkhya philosophy describe ego in a very subtle manner. Ego separates us from the universal consciousness. It gives us identity but also it separates us from higher aspect of reality.

Question that arises from here is that what propels ancient people to know and experiment on this philosophy . According to buddhist text it is pain or suffering . Suffering has given us impetus to understand the higher reality of life. According to Samkhya school of philosophy perception , inference and word are the three means through which knowledge can be attained. Perception can be external and internal. External

perception are derived from senses , internal perception is formed through content of mind.
Now we will discuss about one of the greatest pillar of Indian philosophy that is Yoga. Yoga means union , It is the union of our individual self with the higher cosmic self . Patanjali was the rishi who experimented on the great philosophy of yoga and discovered the greatest knowledge of mysticism. According to yoga when mind with thoughts and five senses stands still and intellect does not waver then this is called the highest path. It involve stillness of the senses and concentration of the mind. it is not thoughtless , heedless and sluggishness . yoga is creation and dissolution.
Next school of Indian philosophy that is very much fascinating and interesting is Vedanta. Meaning of

the word Vedanta is end of vedas . Philosophy of Vedanta discuss about .it talks about expanding our mind and going into deeper realms through meditation and understand the concept of brahman. Meaning of the word brahman is to expand our consciousness to understand higher reality and greater level of existence. Philosophy of Vedanta is made for some very sincere seeker and they should move into isolation to understand the higher phenomenon happening within themselves. Samkhya philosophy is such a great philosophy which regards the universe consisting of two realities . One is consciousness and other is matter . Living being is in such a state in which consciousness is bonded into matter and a bondage is created . This fusion led to emergence of intellect and ego consciousness. According to Samkhya philosophy universe is created by combination of matter and consciousness with various elements of senses , feeling , activity and mind. During the state of imbalance , one or more constituents overwhelm the other , creating a form of bondage , particularily of the mind . The end of this imbalance is called liberation . Best part of Samkhya philosophy is it's depiction of qualities . According to Samkhya there are three qualities in human mind . One is illuminating , other is of activity and third quality comprises of lethargy and negativity . Thus a individual being is constituated of three qualities in one individual being . Negativity can take you down to the recess of lethargy and you daily activity can energies you to normal human being of daily activity. Through meditation we can

upift our inner being into a divine , illuminating consciousness. Thus according to this philosophy our inner being has got various grading . One is succumbing us and another grading is uplifting our entire being.
Ancient philosophers of india have tried to understand higher reality in a different manner. They have developed a entire system of scientific study to understand higher reality. These six system of philosophy are a part of that great tradition. These are orthodox Indian system of philosophy .
Tantra is another great system of Indian philosophy . Meaning of the word tantra is loom or weave like. It means text , theory , system , method , instrument or technique.
According to one text when an action or a thing , once complete , becomes beneficial in several matter to one

matters to one person , or to many people , that is known as tantra. Trantric traditions wants to deal with the inner world to find certain changes that can take us to higher levels of consciousness. The scope of tantra is to find that great higher energy within ourself that is known as kundalini energy . It involves certain technique to find the higher state of consciousness within ourself. Tantric text deals with arousing the kundalini shakti within ourself and this energy can be aroused by various rituals like bija mantra , meditation , sounds. Whatever be the philosophy , ultimate aim is to find liberation . Best part of tantric philosophy is that both the worldly success and enlightment is achievable and this world need not to be shunned to achieve enlightment.

To understand the spiritual philosophy , the most important concept is understanding of nadis and chakras. There are three principle nadis within us , ida , pingala and shushumna. Shushumna nadi is mostly blocked with our fear , apprehension and thoughts. We operate in our normal world with only ida and pingala . Ida nadi is for work of higher energy state while pingala nadi is for that kind of work which require calmness and peace. To go into spiritual ecstasy our mind should move into shushumna nadi . In shushumna nadi our mind moves into higher state of consciousness .In that higher state mind reaches expanded state of awareness . This is such a wonderful state which takes us into best of our being.

Same kind of ecstasy is experienced in sexual energy state but the direction is downward.

In deep meditative practices these energy moves in upward state and we experience ocean of bliss and happiness. All the desires of humanity can be achieved in that higher state .only we have to increase the awareness within ourself .Main purpose of existence of human being in this world is desire. Desire can be of many kind desire of attaining money ,power and possession is very concrete to our existence .Again there can be desire of peace, liberation and bliss.These all desires can be satisfied in deeper state of consciousness . Always remember that spirituality is just not about liberation ,it is also about attaining materialistic pursuits in life

.Six system of Indian philosophy wants to teach about that .
It is about how to expand our inner being and take it to new higher dimension .It espouses dualism between consciousnesss and matter . Body is form in which consciousness is bound to matter.This fusion has led to emergence of intellect and ego. Sankhya philosophy wants to tell us about three qualities one is illuminating other is passionate and third one is lethargic. The interplay of these three qualities determines character of someone .
Samkhya theories the pluralism of souls who pocess consciousness , but it denies the existence of god. It is a type of atheistic philosophy. It opens the doorway of Indian philosophy which talks about three kind of suffering , one is physical , other is spiritual and third one is

mental . Aim of life is to get free from these three kind of suffering and be free.

Other philosophy that is yoga accepts the concept of personal god . It says that there are three ways of attain knowledge , one is perception ,other is inference and third one is word . Yoga is form of experimental mysticism .

Vaisesika metaphysical premises beliefs that reality is composed of four substances air, water, earth and fire. Each of these four are of two types atomic and composite . What we see is composite and what we do not see is atomic .

The vedant school is build upon the teachings of upnishad and bramhasutra and is most developed . Brahman is something that is ever expanding in nature and wants to go in the journey of expansiveness . There is another word in vedant known as advaita . It means not two,sole,unity it tells about monism, that is reality is interconnected oneness.

According to this school of Vedanta ,all reality is brahman , and there exist nothing whatsoever which is brahman. Its metaphysics includes the concept of maya and atman.

CHAPTER FOUR

HOW TO ACHIEVE OUR DESIRE?

Purpose of existence of human being is to achieve the desire that they have in there mind . Achieving our desire needs lots of hard work , discipline and patience. But there are some unmanifested reality that is also responsible for manifestion of desire. Satisfaction of desire needs lots of unmanifested components . In deep state of meditation our desires are satisfied in more faster manner . Universe listens to the mind which is silent and powerful. This mind can materialise everything . A distracted and troubled mind can not perceive what it wants . In deep state of silence nature listen to us in more sincere manner .

This silent and expanded mind itself a desired entity . Many civilisation from centuaries are desiring this higher state of consciousness. In our mental world we live in a box . We are not able to think out of the box . The reality within this box is very much harsh . When we think out of the box then we can manifest anything from the subtle nature of unmanifested energy. It looks very much miraculous and divine but it is really true . But the effort that is needed is very massive . A human being should try to meditate harder and should visualise his desires . This deeper visualisation has the power to manifest itself . Imagination is a greater force within ourself which has got the great potency . It is like every word has a form . Form that is associated with a word is a stronger entity .

So if you want to manifest anything in your life then you should try to imagine that desire within yourself daily . This visualisation should be realised in a very concrete manner. So go deeper and deeper , you will become master of the mind you have . Mastering the mind will give you asset to master the material world also.

This mastered mind can attain anything for himself. Entire purpose of our existence can be solved through deep practices of meditation . whether you want peace , happiness , bliss or material . anything can be achieved through this higher science of manifestation .

Ancients have deviced various technique to settle down there mind . Settled mind is such apowerful entity that it can do anything . They have developed various psychological process of manifestation . It is known as command over mind and matter. These are the realities which are not visible through common eyes but through deeper realisation these things can be achieved.

To manifest anything first of all we should cross conditioning of mind. Mind is always conditioned in it's form of thoughts and images. In deep absorption of mind in certain pleasurable things can take our mind out of this conditioning . Peace and bliss is very essential part of this freedom .

There is soo much negativity , violence and distruction in this world . In this situation it become very difficult to achieve something positive in our inner world . Only deep level of understanding of our inner world can give us this kind of freedom . Always remember that this kind of mind is goal of life. Entire world is dream creation of higher reality , we are living in a dream of somebody else . So we have to woke up to know our real nature, Our real nature is the life that we are craving always . This kind of peaceful and blissful life can be achievable by everyone.

In spirituality inner reality is far more greater than external reality. Both external and internal world are inter realate with each other. Inner consciousness expands and become the part of external world. In this world things become very easy for us to manifest.

Our mind has soo much great potential and this potential can be realised in deep state of meditation and mysticism . We are not the mere entity of conditioning of life , we are far more greater than our tiny bodies . Our mind is far more greater than external situation .We can overcome any situation in life and become free to attain our real nature that is divinity.

www.ingramcontent.com/pod-product-compliance
Lightning Source LLC
LaVergne TN
LVHW050336160826
845677LV00014B/3641